This book belongs to:

_ _ _ _ _ _ _ _ _

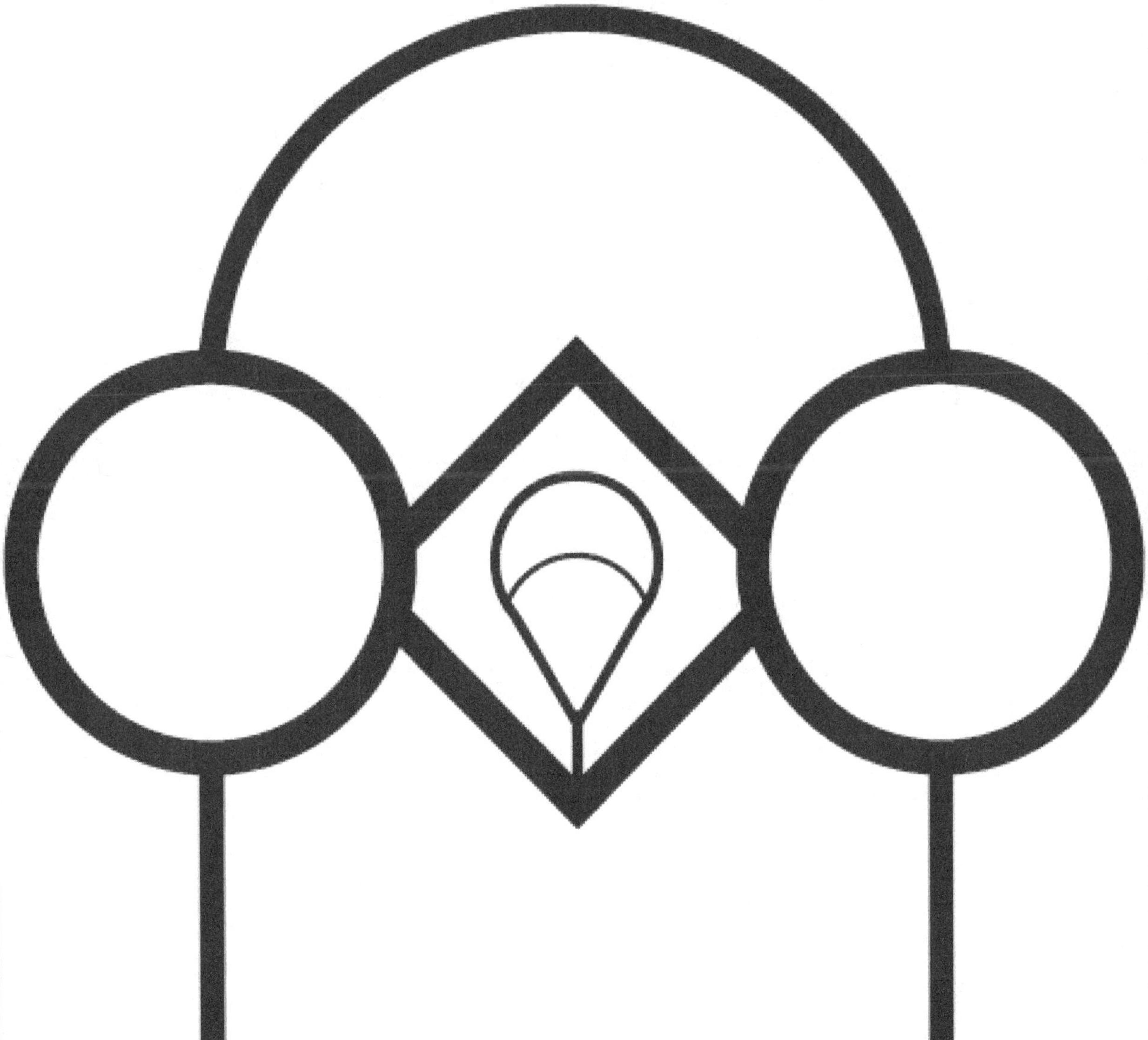

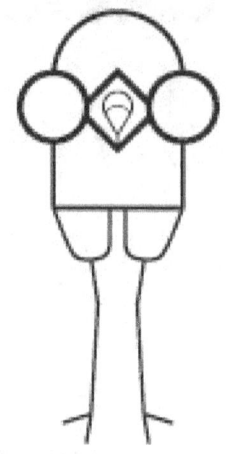

Copyright © 2020

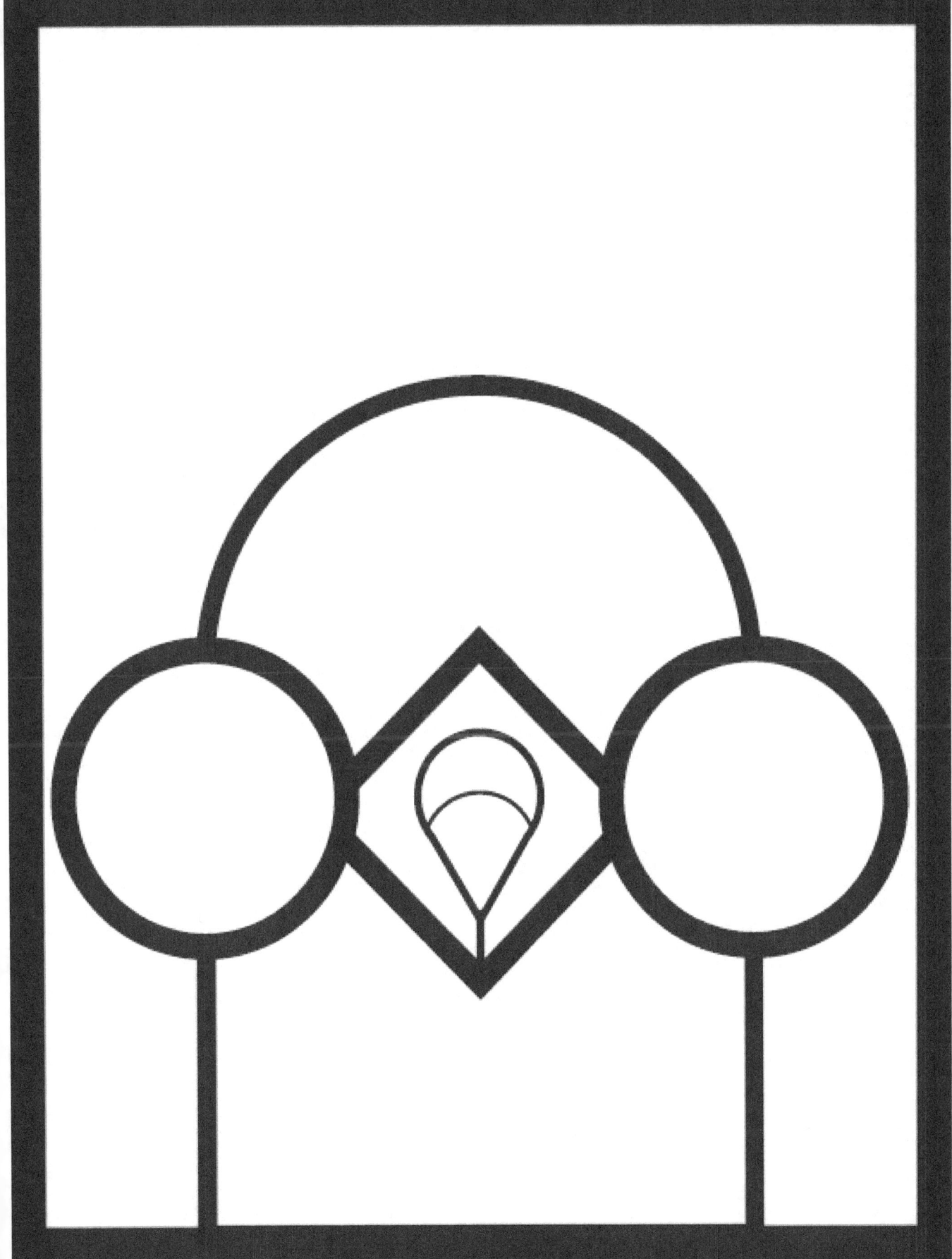

Burdie

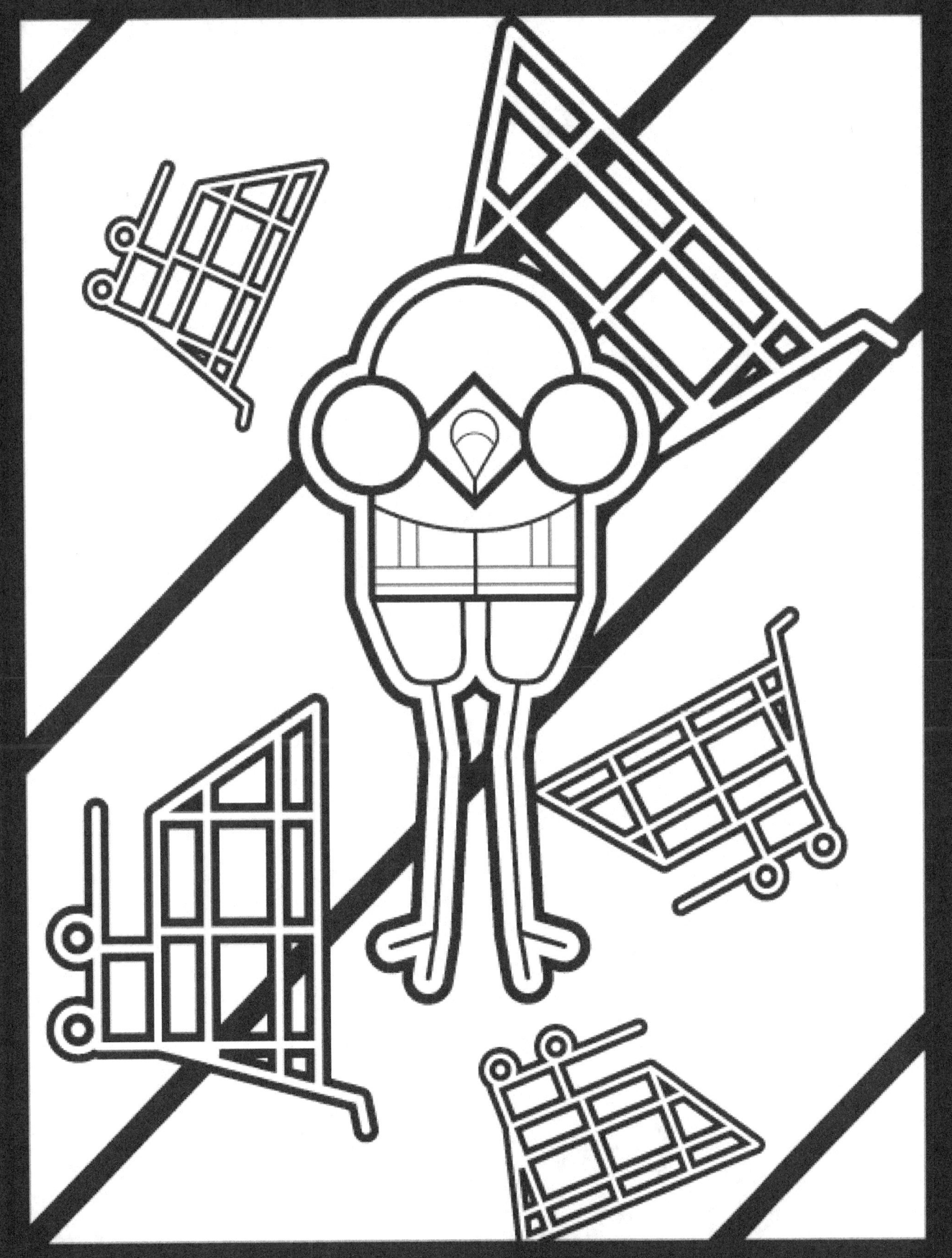

Cart Burd

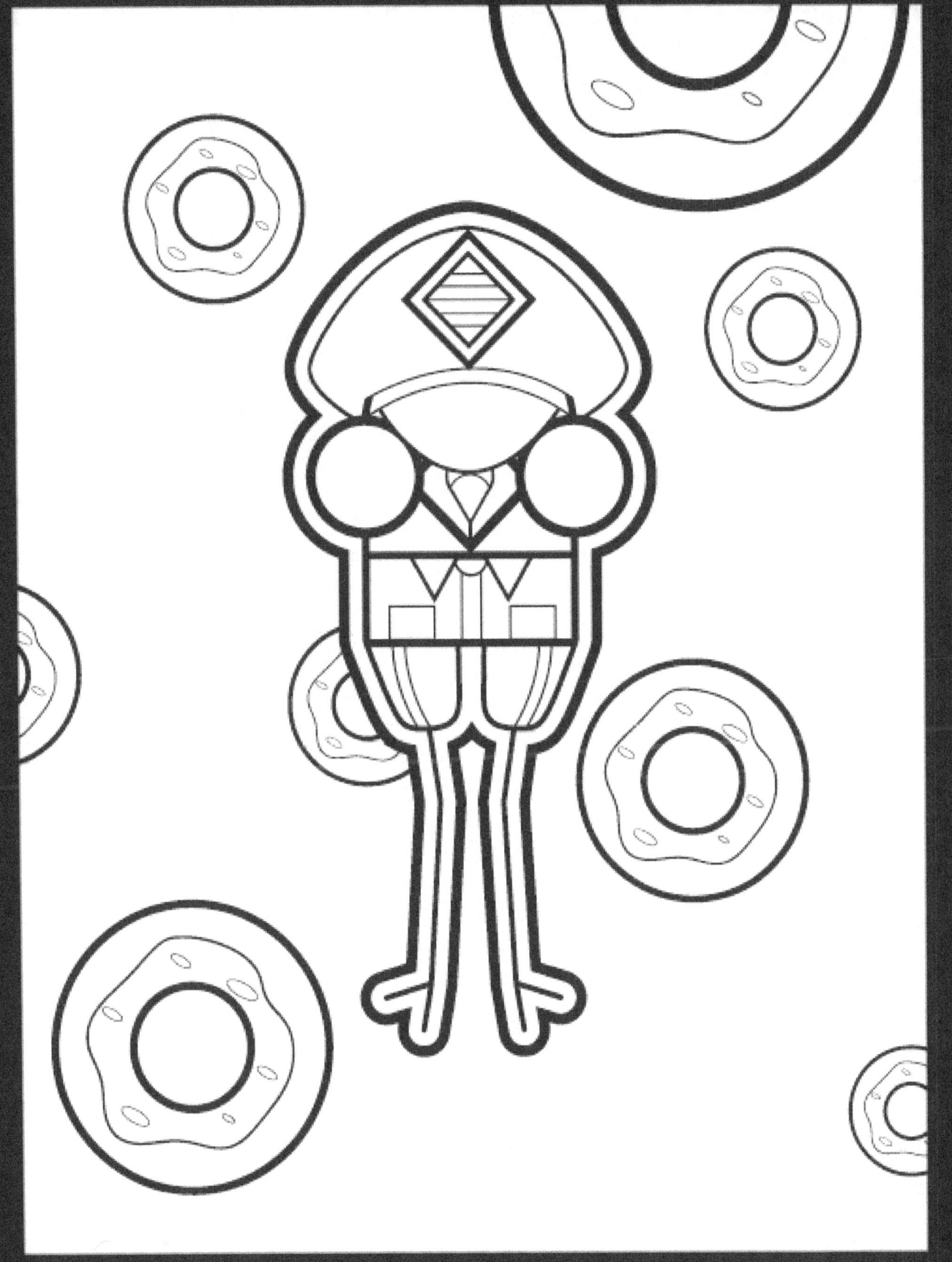

Officer Burd

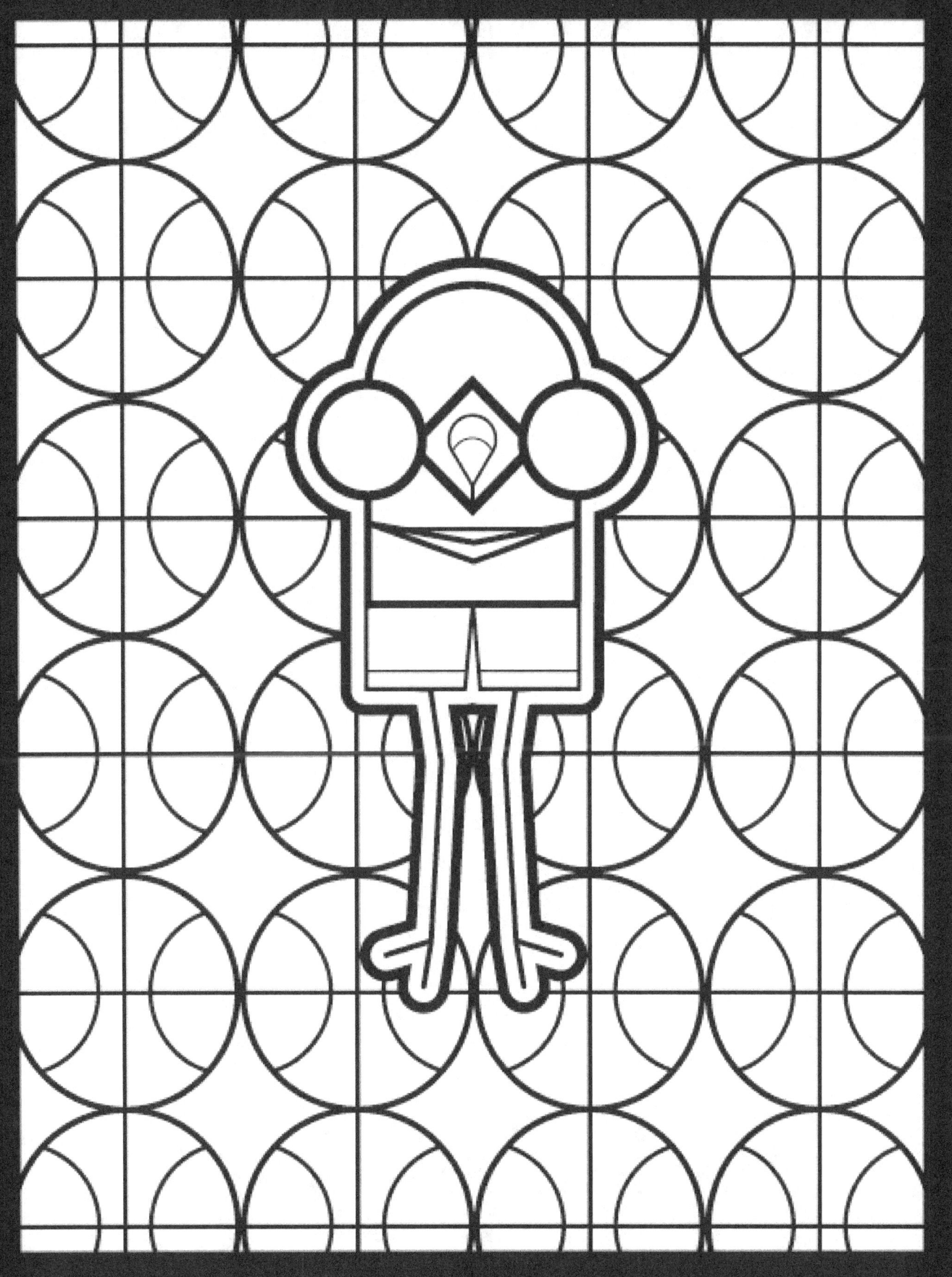

Basketball Burd

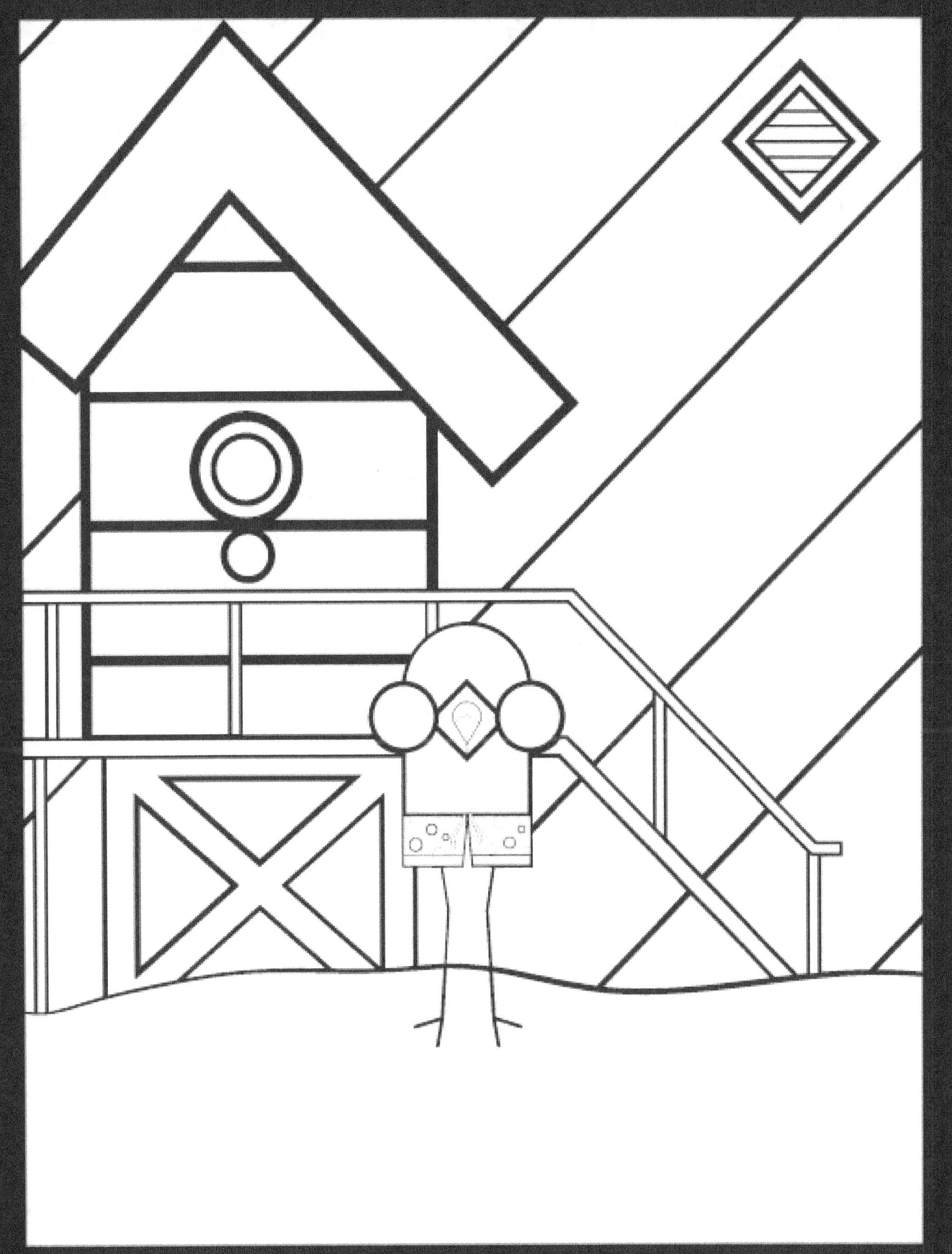

Lifeguard Burd

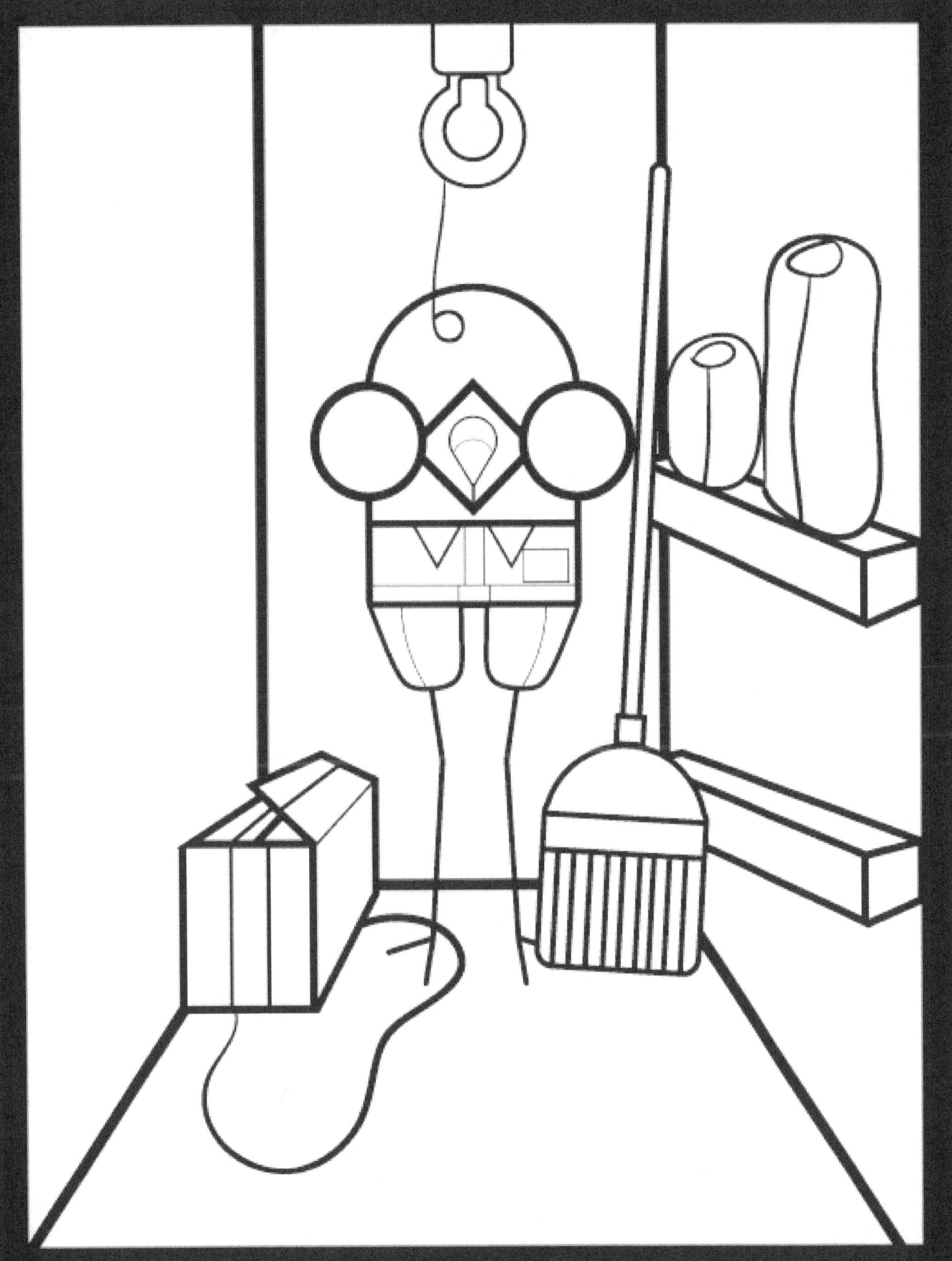

Janitor Burd

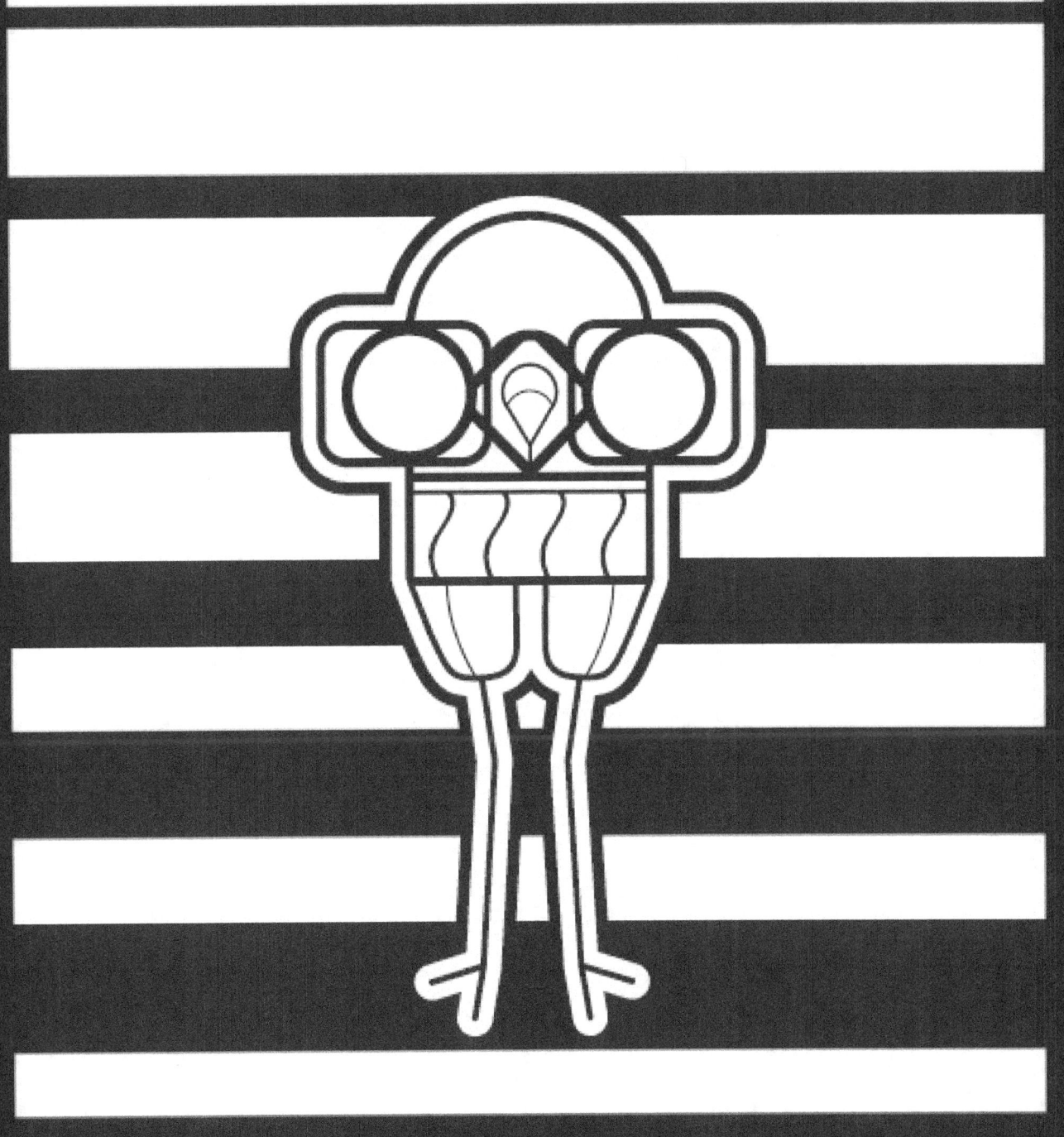

Therapist Burd

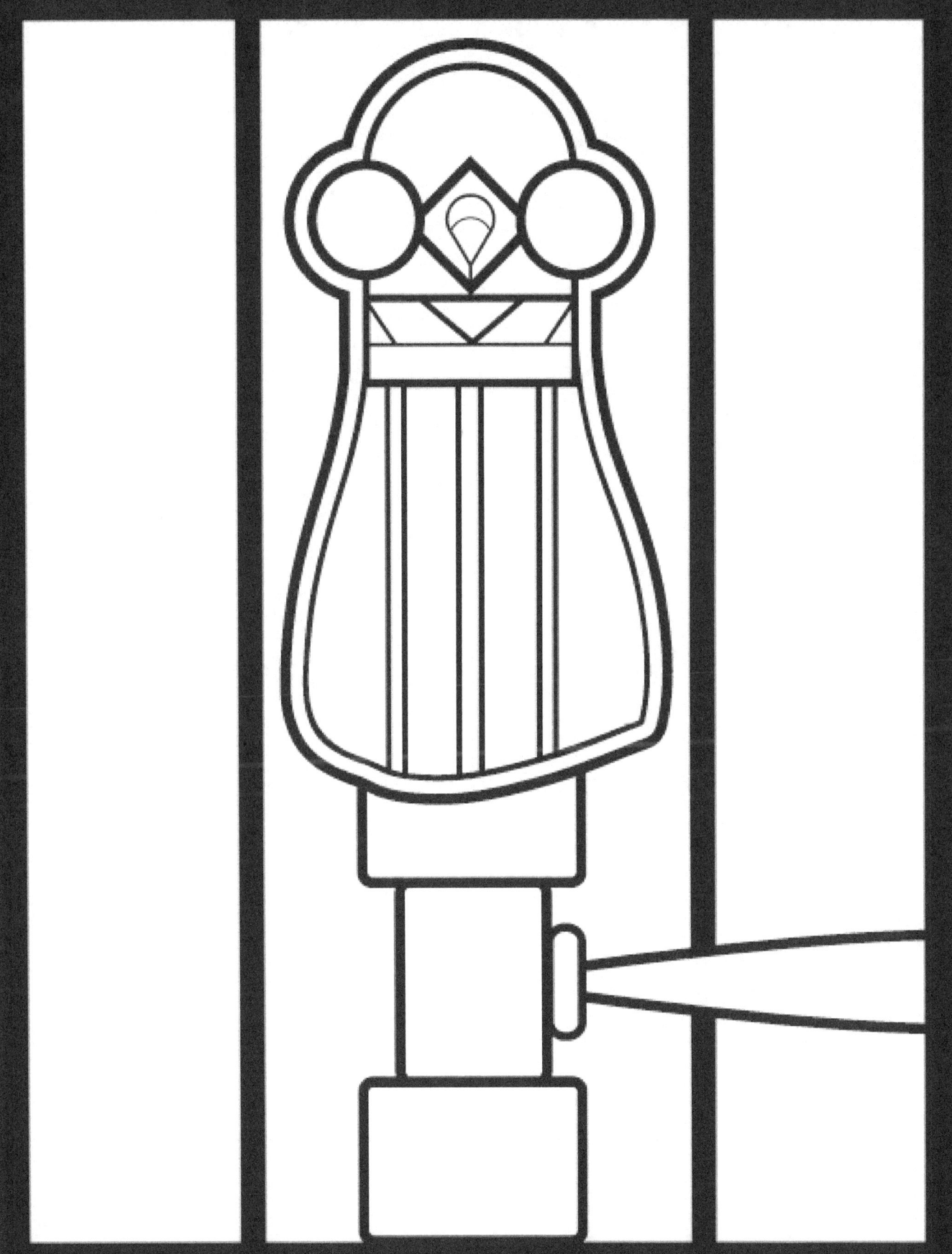

Law Burd

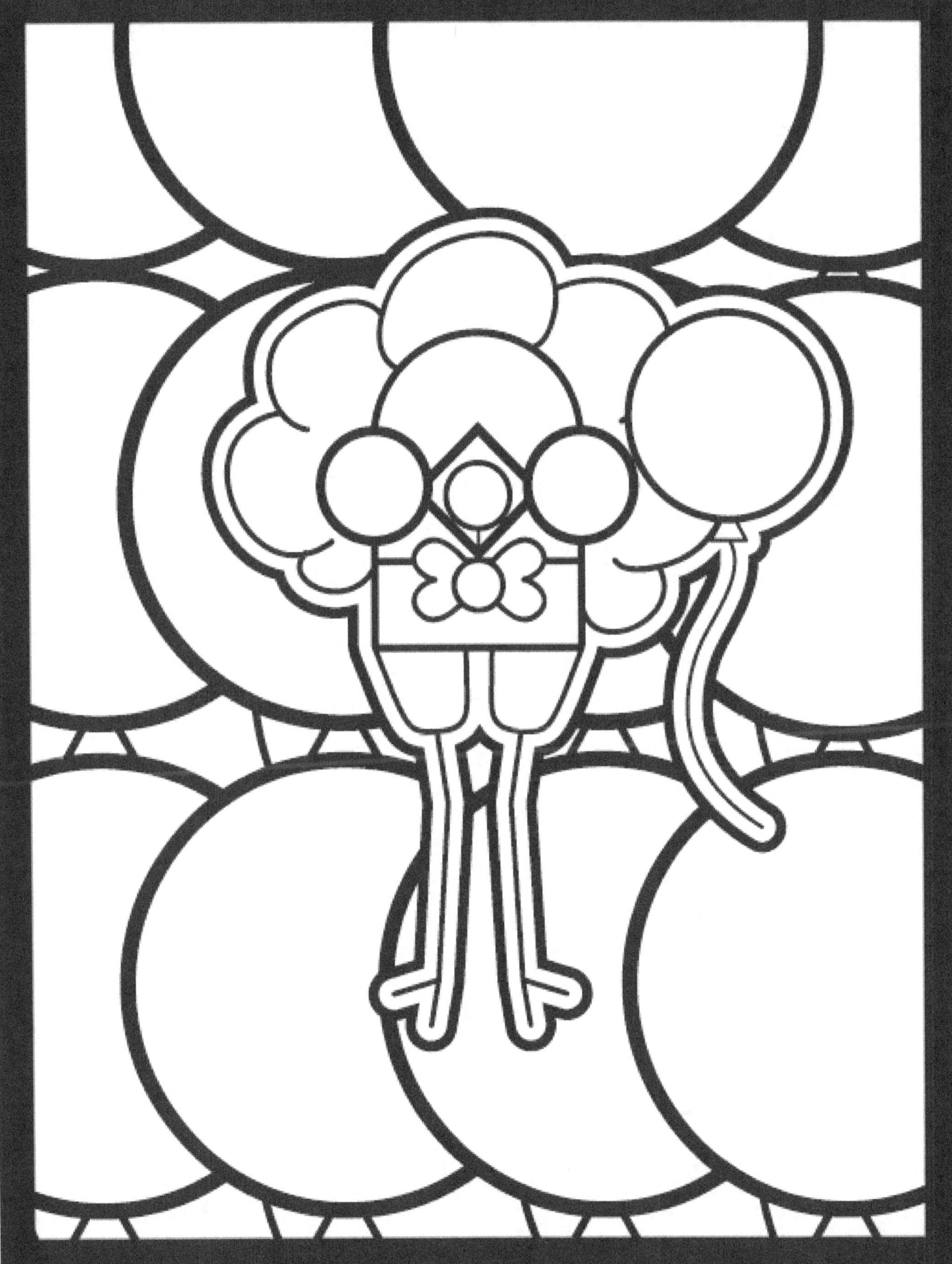

Clown Burd

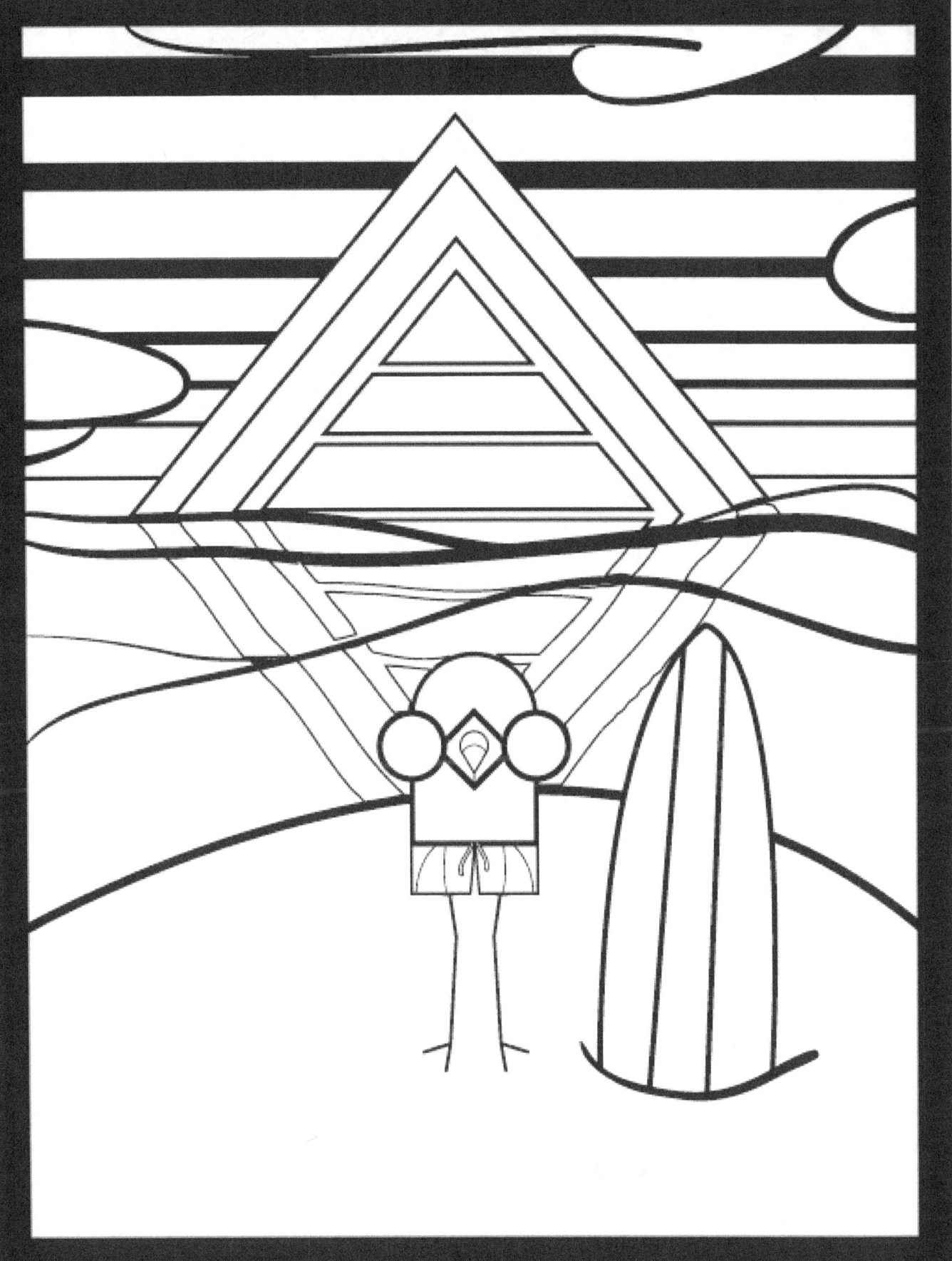

Surfer Burd

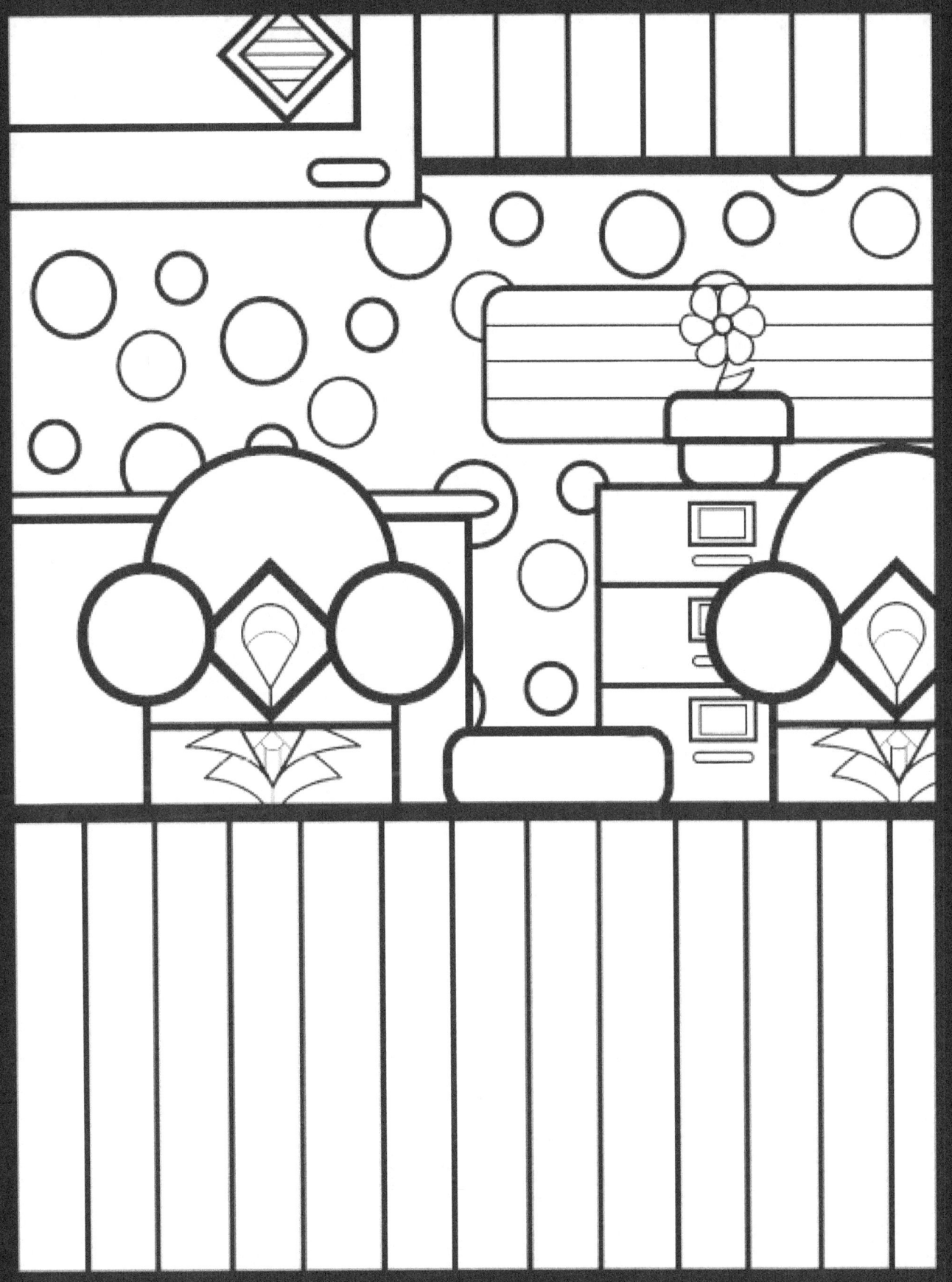

Bank Burd

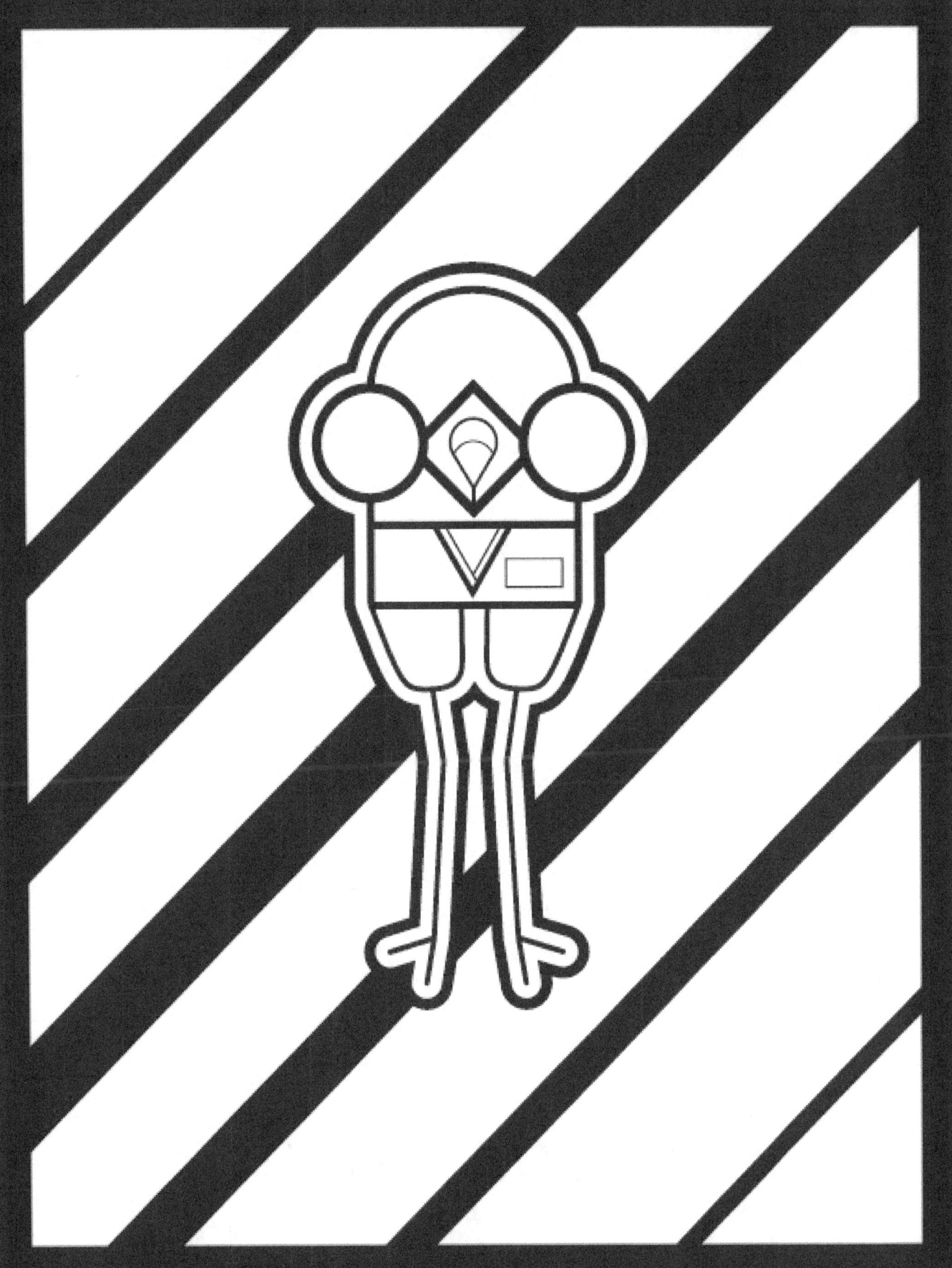

Nurse Burd

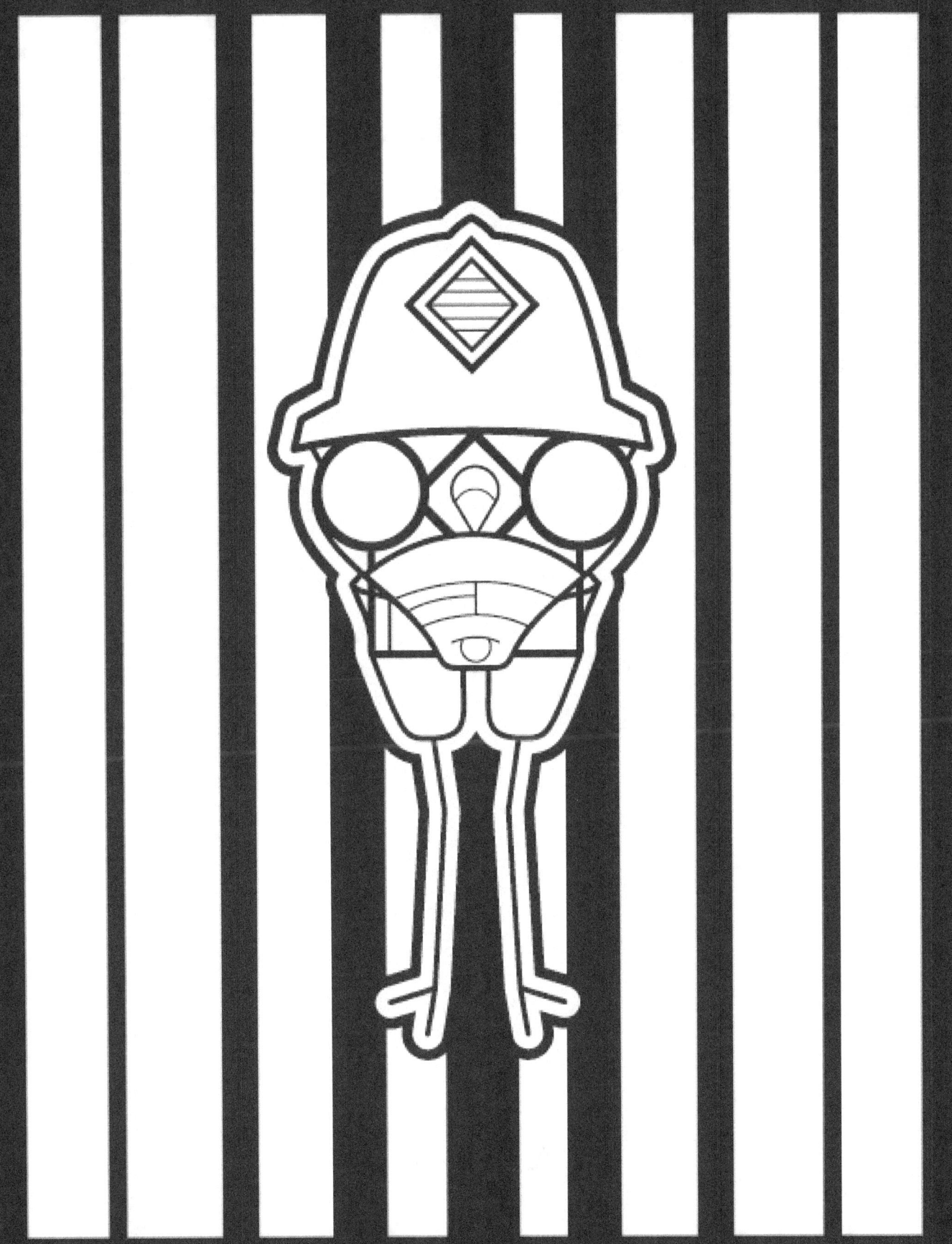

Fire Burd

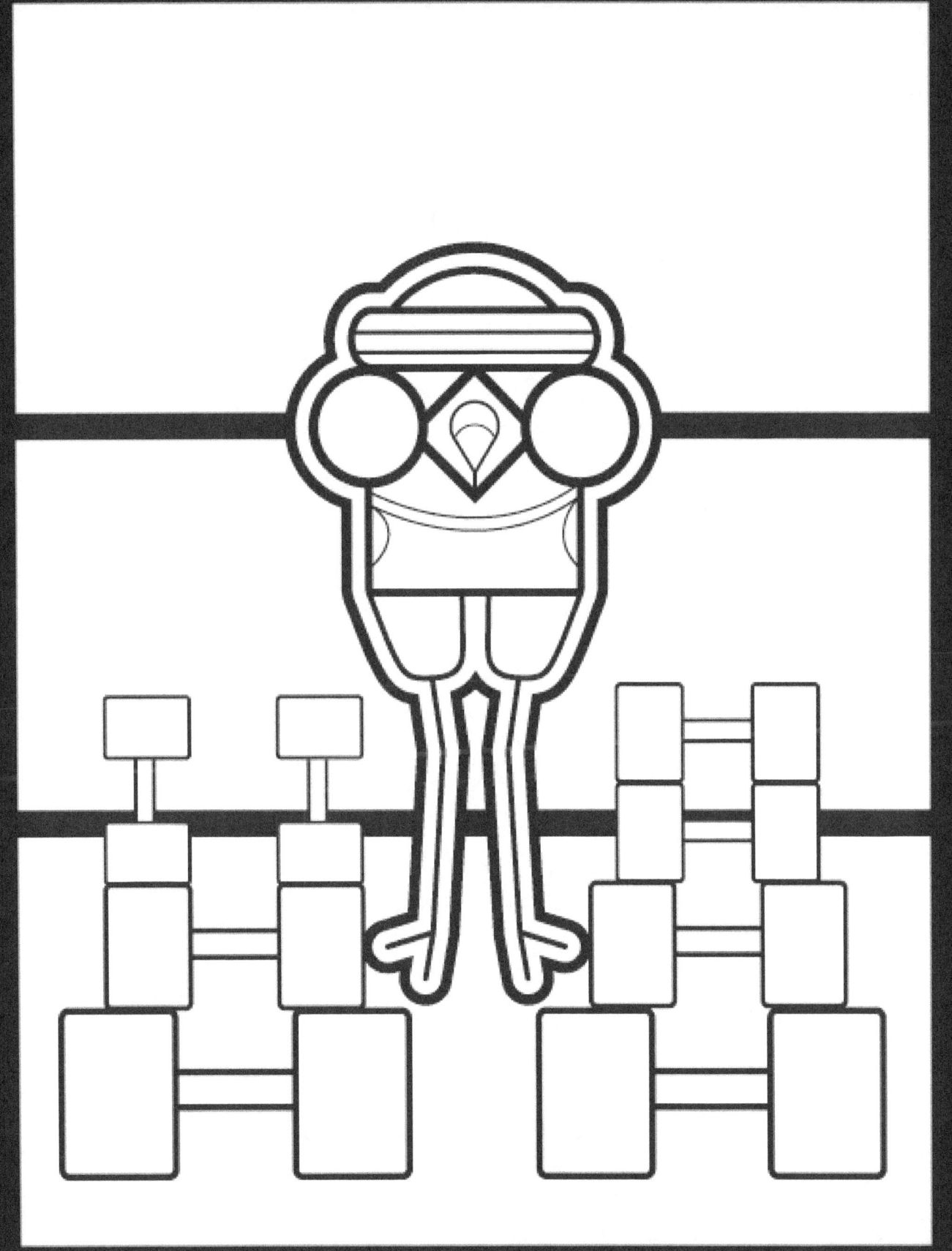

Gym Burd

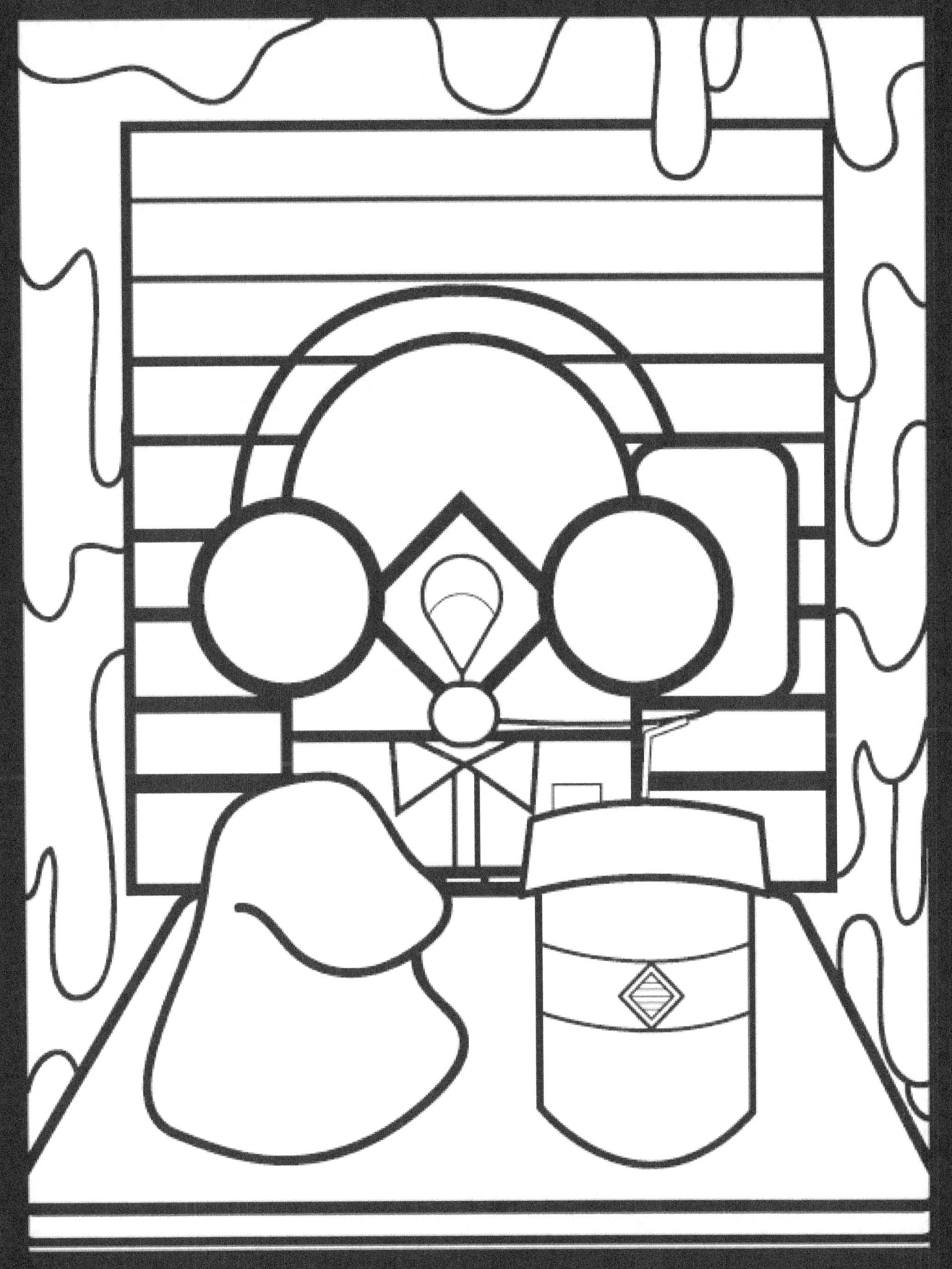

Food Burd

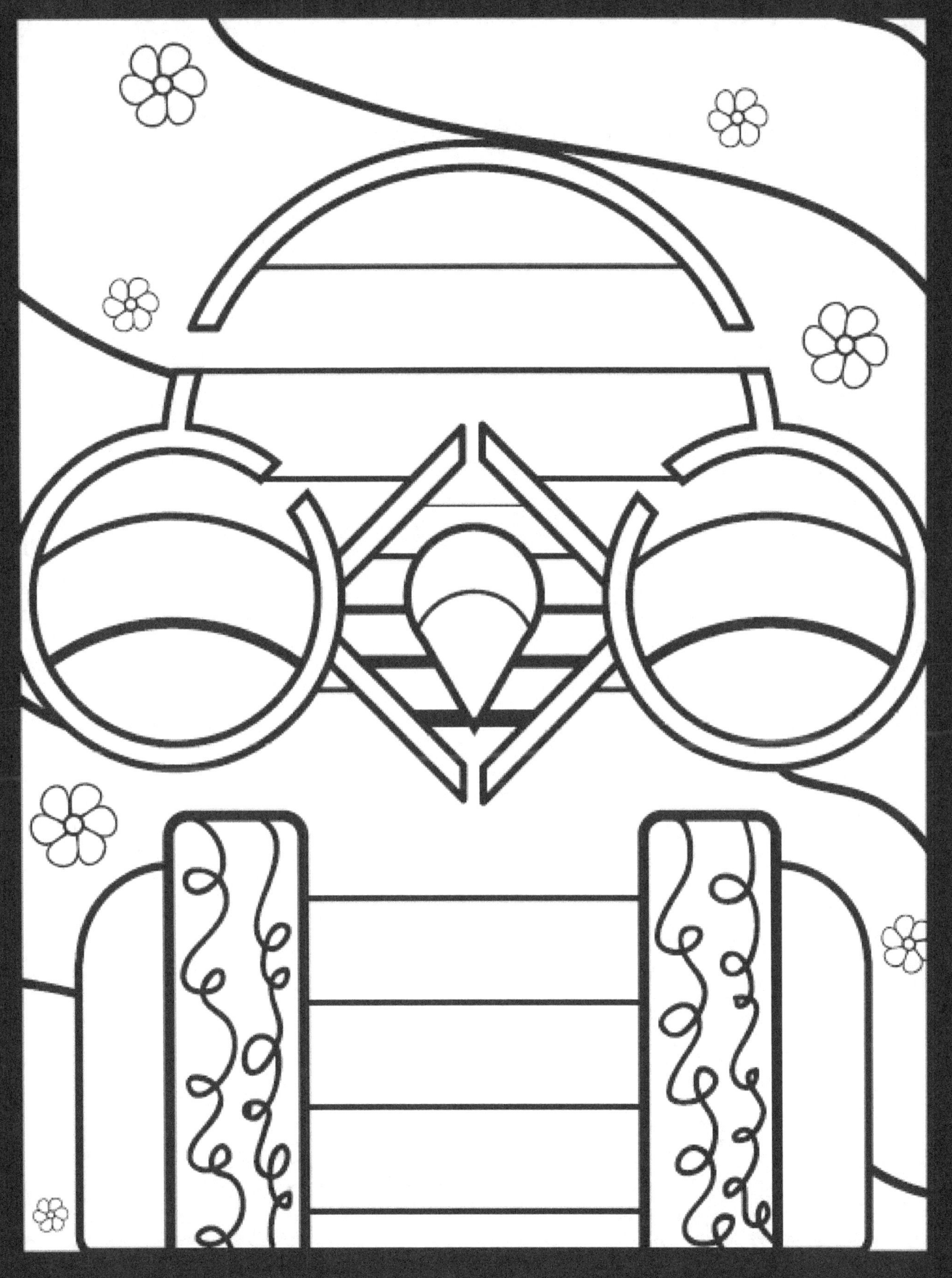

Burd Garden

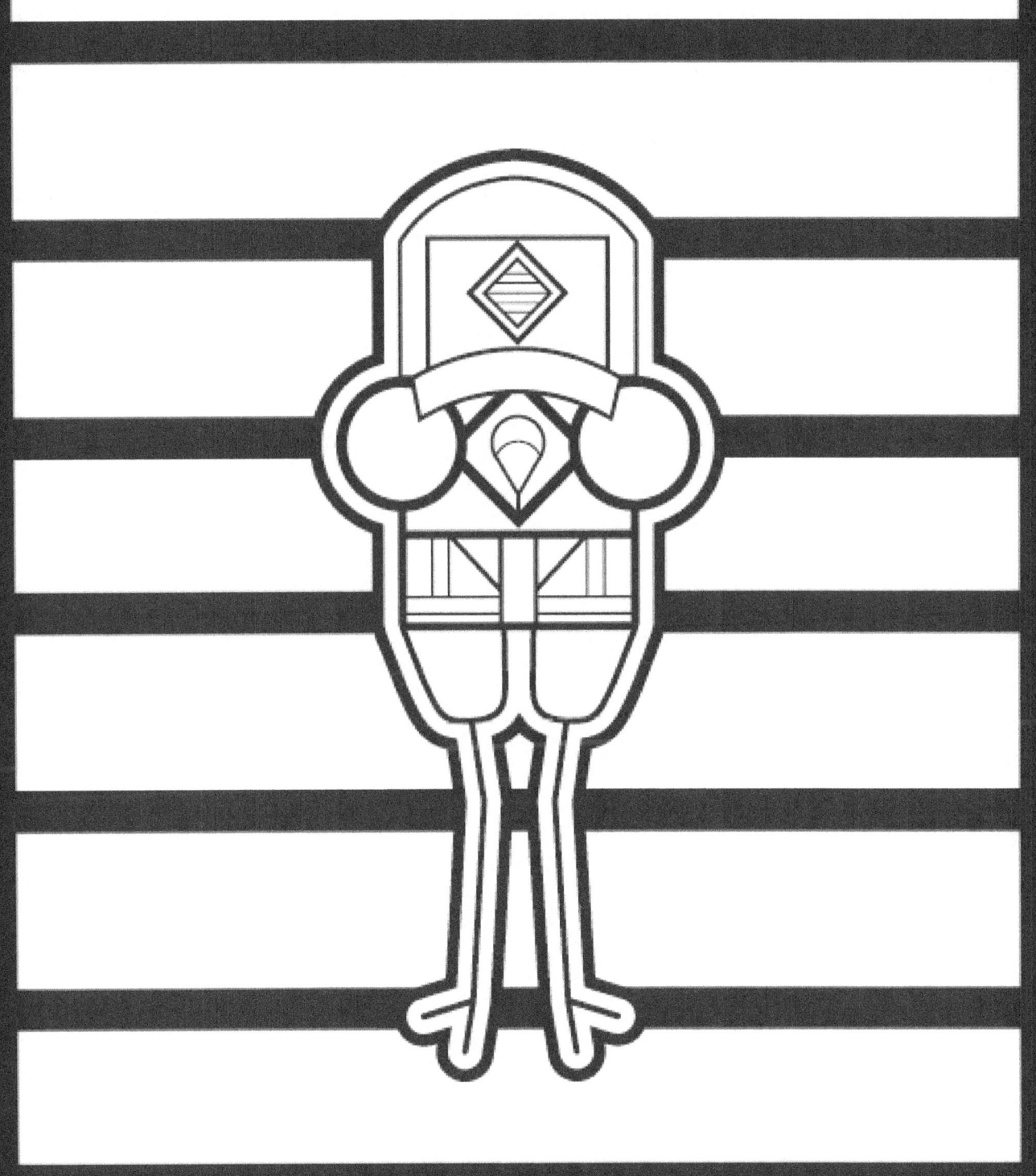

Trucker Burd

Detective Burd

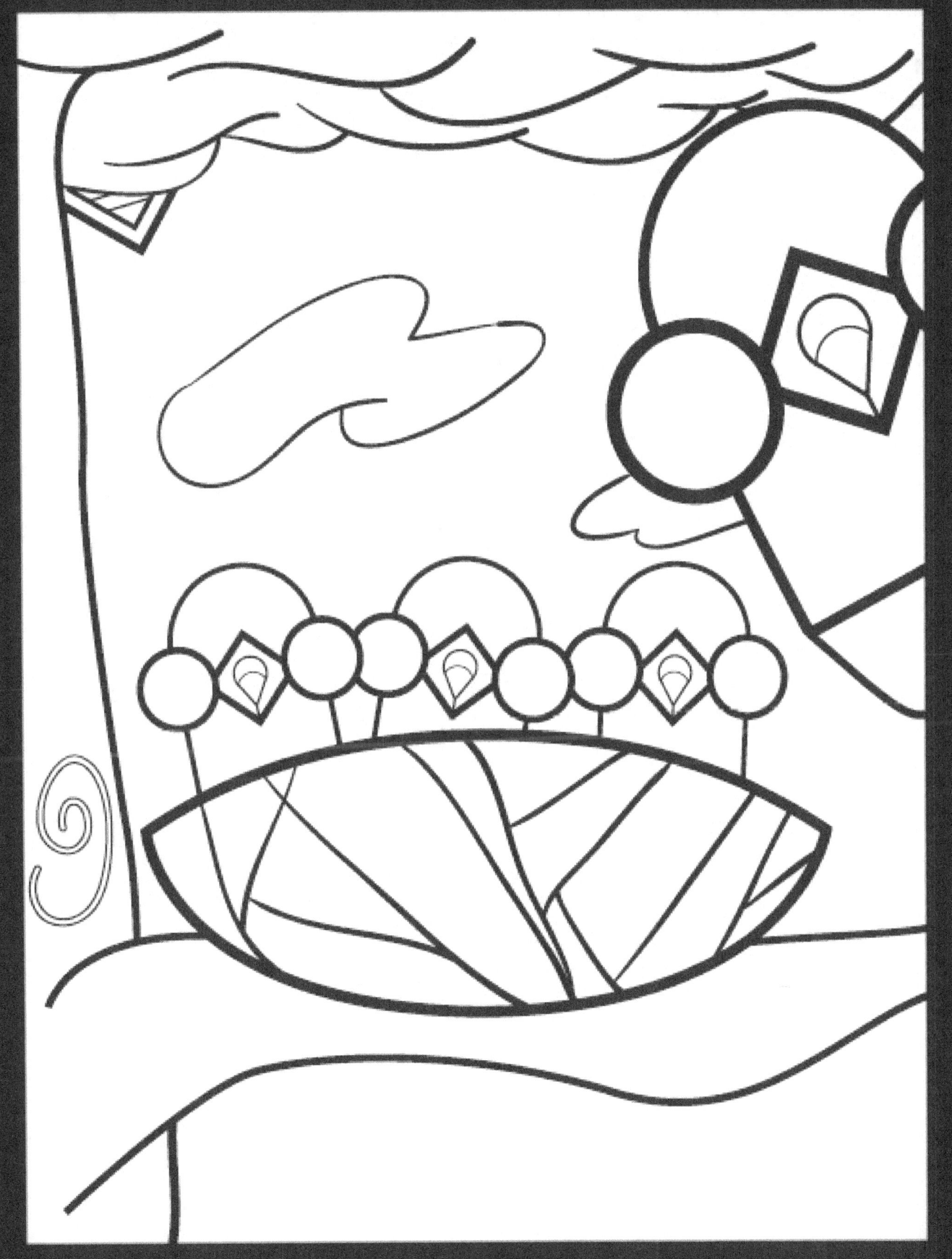

Burd Nest

5-Day Forecast

BurdNews

MOA 8

FRI	SAT	SUN	MON	TUE
32	50	64		
25	40	5		

COMING UP!!!

6:30

Two birds? One stone?

Burd News

5-Day Forecast

FRI	SAT	SUN	MON	TUE
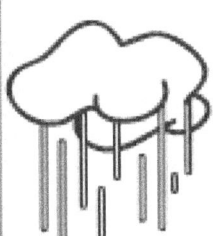	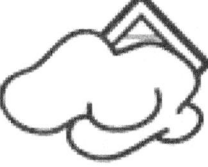	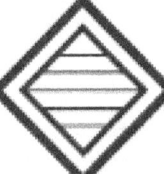		
32	50	64		
25	40	5		

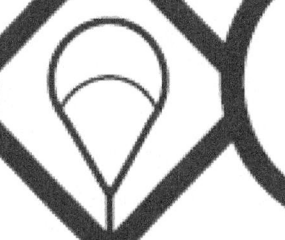

COMING UP!!!

6:30

Two birds? One stone?

Burd News Extra

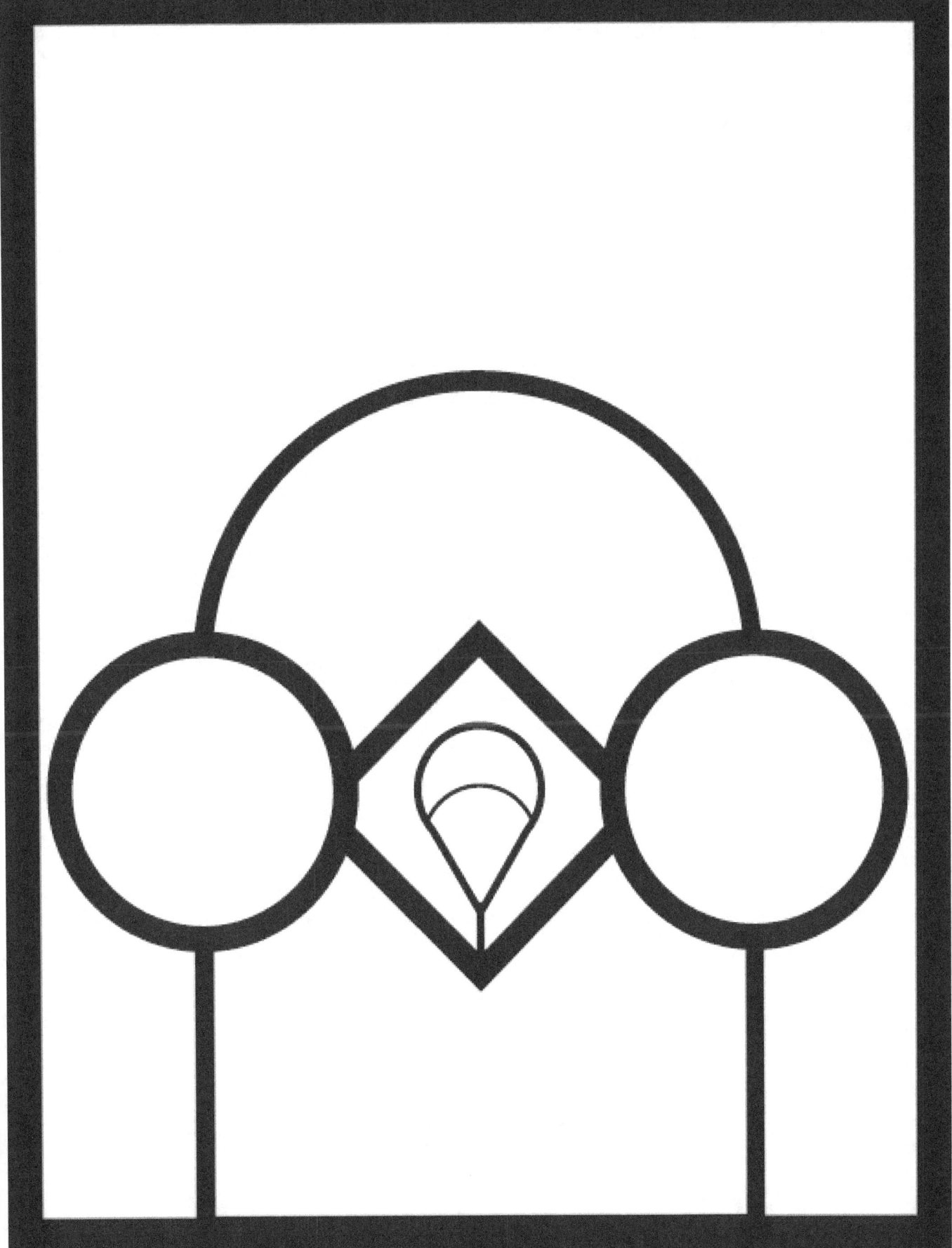

Burdie

Burd Crowd

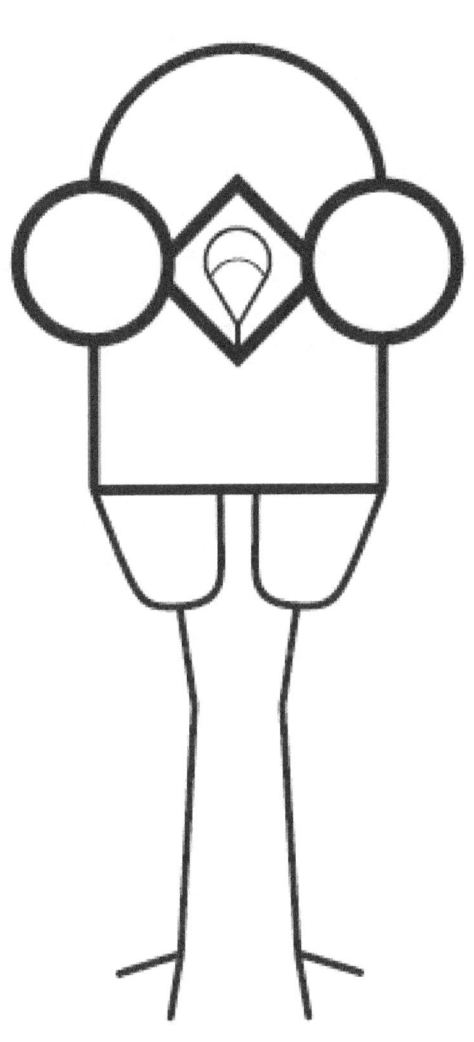

Lone Burd